**Other Cambridge Reading books
you may enjoy**

The Princess and the Pea
J. Burchett and S. Vogler

A Walk with Granny
Nigel Gray

A Door to Secrets
Tony Mitton

Carnival
Grace Hallworth

**Other books by Sally Grindley
you may enjoy**

Peter's Place

Polar Star

Why is the Sky Blue?

CHIMBA was only six, but he loved football. He thought football, he talked football, and he dreamed of football every night.

Chimba played football with anything he could find. He kicked stones and mango fruits, rolled up pieces of paper, even a bit of old sponge. He scored goals against imaginary keepers standing between goalposts made of buckets.

He watched football too. He watched
the crowd of bigger boys who played every
day on the wasteground close to his home.
He watched because they wouldn't let him
play.

"You're too young," they said. "You're
not good enough," they said. "You'll get
hurt," they said.

He was good enough. He knew he was.
But they didn't want him, so he played on
his own, every hour of every day, when he
wasn't at school or running errands for his
mother.

In just a few weeks, Chimba would be seven. He longed to have a proper football for his birthday, but he knew his parents could not afford it. They worked hard on their smallholding, but years of drought had made it difficult for them to do much more than keep their family fed and clothed. All Chimba could expect was a special cake and perhaps some chocolate.

But when the day came, a surprise
visitor knocked at the door. Chimba
opened it to his smiling uncle, who had
just arrived back from a trip overseas.
Under his arm he carried a large parcel
wrapped in brightly coloured paper.

Chimba dared not think it might be for him, but when his uncle handed it to him and said, "Happy birthday, Chimba," he grabbed it excitedly and ripped the paper off. It was a football, a brand-new, white leather football. Chimba held it to his nose and smelt the leathery smell. He hugged it to his chest and smiled the biggest smile.

He threw himself at his uncle and thanked him, thanked him, thanked him.

Then he rushed into the yard and began to kick his football around. His uncle followed him, and together they dribbled and passed and tackled all afternoon. It wasn't long before all the boys of the village were watching. None of them had a real football and they longed to join in.

The next morning, Chimba opened the
door to Akim, leader of the village boys.

"Do you want to play football with us?"
he asked Chimba.

Chimba was thrilled. He knew they wanted him to play because they wanted to use his ball, but he didn't mind. As long as he could play, nothing else mattered.

He ran with Akim to the wasteground to the cheers of the other boys.

The game began. Chimba ran and passed and headed. He dribbled and volleyed and lobbed and played the game of his life.

And then he shot at goal, a huge kick,
a mighty kick, a kick that carried the ball
up, up and over the goalmouth, over the
marula bushes, over into the swirling
waters of the great river.

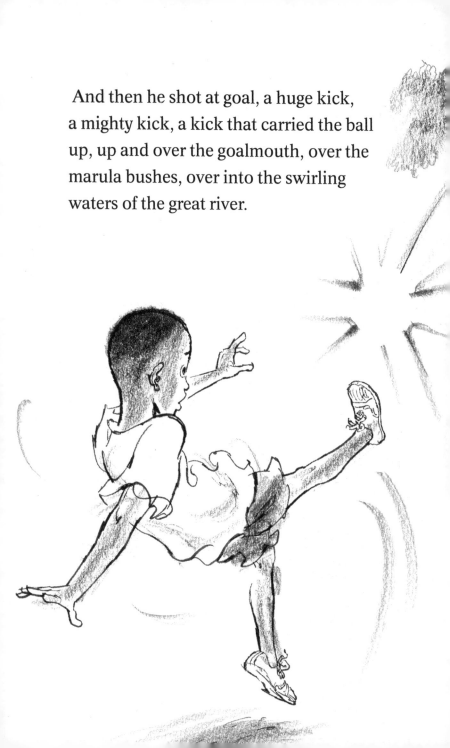

The boys watched in amazement, then horror, then they sprinted to the water's edge, only to see Chimba's ball being carried swiftly along, already too far away for them to reach it.

Chimba ran back home in tears. He had lost his brand-new ball, the best present he had ever had. And he had lost the chance of playing again with the other boys from the village. His uncle tried to cheer him up by saying he would bring him another ball the next time he visited, but Chimba knew his uncle could only visit once or twice a year.

When he went to bed that night, he
wished over and over that he hadn't
kicked the ball so hard. He had wanted so
much to score a goal to prove that he was
good enough to play with the older boys.
Now they would never invite him again
and he would be back to playing on his
own.

He was woken the next morning by his mother's voice calling him to come to the door. He pulled on his clothes and ran out of the house. Akim stood there, arms behind his back.

"We're sorry about your ball," he said, "but we want you to come and play with us. We've got a match next week against the next village and we want you to play midfield for our team."

Chimba couldn't believe his ears. They wanted him to play even without his football!

Then Akim brought out a football from behind his back. Chimba couldn't believe his eyes. It was his brand new ball!

"But how – ?" Chimba began.

"It got caught in some weeds further along the river. I went looking for it, and managed to fish it out."

Chimba couldn't thank Akim enough.

He took his ball and hugged it tight.

"I'll be more careful with it today," he said.

But Akim said, "Let's not play with your ball for practice games. We don't want to lose it again. Save it for big games. Perhaps we could use it for the match next Saturday?"

Chimba rushed to tell his uncle.

For the whole of the following week, Chimba could think about nothing except the big match. He snatched every moment he could to practise in the back yard with his uncle. And in the evenings he ran over to the wasteground to practise with the rest of the team.

When Saturday finally arrived, Chimba was almost paralysed with excitement and fear. He polished his brand new football boots for the umpteenth time, and stared across at the wasteground, where in a very short time the match would begin.

"What if I'm no good?" he said to his uncle, over and over again.

"You'll be fine," said his uncle. "I'll be watching you, and you'll be fine."

And now it was time to go. When they reached the wasteground, the rest of the team ran over to greet them and wished Chimba good luck. Chimba carried his ball proudly to the centre spot, and the game began. It was a hard game, a rough game. The other team seemed so much bigger than his own team, but Chimba soon showed that size wasn't everything.

He ran and he passed and he dribbled
and he lobbed and he volleyed, and he
cheered and cheered when Akim scored a
goal from a pass that he had given him.
But then the other team equalised, and
time was running out. Chimba ran with
his brand new ball, neatly side-stepping
every challenge that threatened to stop
him in his tracks.

Then he unleashed a huge kick, a mighty kick, a kick that carried the ball up, up and over the goalkeeper's head, into the back of the rickety goal. A few seconds later, the final whistle blew.

Cities, Towns and Villages

Jen Green

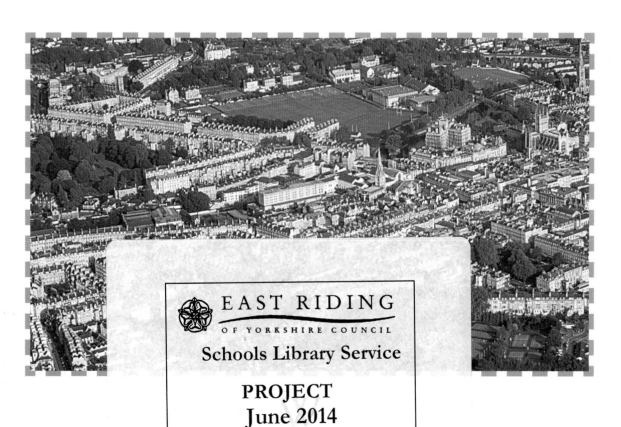

FRANKLIN WATTS
LONDON • SYDNEY

This edition published in 2012
by Franklin Watts

Copyright © Franklin Watts 2012

Franklin Watts
338 Euston Road
London NW1 3BH

Franklin Watts Australia
Level 17/207 Kent Street
Sydney, NSW 2000

Series editor: Sarah Peutrill
Art director: Jonathan Hair
Design: White Design
Additional map illustrations: John Alston
Consultant: Steve Watts

A CIP catalogue record for this book is available
from the British Library.

Dewey number: 526.09141
ISBN: 978 1 4451 0932 9

Printed in China

Franklin Watts is a division of Hachette Children's
Books, an Hachette Livre UK company.

www.hachette.co.uk

Picture credits:
Chris Andrews/Corbis: 1,19. Graham Bell/PD:13.
Jason Hawkes/Corbis: front cover r, 23. Jason
Hawkes/Image Bank/Getty Images: 27. Ordnance
Survey © Crown copyright 2007: front cover l.
Ordnance Survey © Crown copyright 2007
supplied by mapsinternational.co.uk: 9, 10, 14,
17, 21, 22, 24, 28, 29. Reuters/Corbis: 25. G R
Richardson/Superstock: 7. Simmons
Aerofilms/Getty Images: 15. Sandy
Stockwell/LAP/Corbis: 11, 16, 20. Stone/Getty
Images: 5. Woodmansterne/Topfoto: 8, 18. Every
attempt has been made to clear copyright. Should
there be any inadvertent omission please apply to
the publisher for rectification.

Note to parents and teachers: Every effort has
been made by the Publishers to ensure that these
websites are suitable for children, that they are of
the highest educational value, and that they
contain no inappropriate or offensive material.
However, because of the nature of the Internet,
it is impossible to guarantee that the contents of
these sites will not be altered. We strongly advise
that Internet access is supervised by a
responsible adult.